J. M. W. TURNER
1775-1851

The illustrations in this book provide a carefully balanced chrono-
logical survey of J. M. W. Turner's development and achievement as a
painter in oils and water-colours. The accompanying text uses these
illustrations as links in telling the story of Turner's remarkable career,
and describes and analyses the various stages of his art. This progressed
from the competent but unoriginal water-colours and paintings of the
1790's to a remarkable mastery of the traditional naturalistic and
classical landscape styles, and finally to the great and inspired paintings
of the 1830's and 40's, in which the artist revealed his genius in a deep
understanding of problems of light, colour and form.

LUKE HERRMANN

J. M. W. TURNER

1775-1851

METHUEN & CO LTD

36 ESSEX STREET · STRAND · LONDON WC2

First published 1963
© 1963 *Luke Herrmann*
Printed in Great Britain
by the Shenval Press
London, Hertford and Harlow
Cat No 2/2611/28 (*Paperback*)
2/2697/28 (*Hardbound*)

PLATES

The engraving reproduced on this page is one of Turner's illustrations to Samuel Rogers's *Italy* (1830), and that on page 43 to Rogers's *Poems* (1834).

J. M. W. Turner began his artistic studies in the year of the French Revolution. He died in 1851, a few months after the closing of the Great Exhibition. Thus his working life spanned a period of vital and rapid political, economic and social development. It was also a period which saw great changes in the field of painting, particularly in England. When Turner became a student at the Royal Academy its President was Sir Joshua Reynolds, who was still very much the dominant figure among the painters of the day. Turner's career coincided with those of Sir Thomas Lawrence, William Blake, John Constable and Samuel Palmer, and in the year of his death the Pre-Raphaelites were just coming to the fore. In this momentous period Turner, through the dedicated and inspired pursuit of his art, ranks as one of the outstanding men of the time.

Turner was essentially a landscape painter, and even in his great historical canvases it is his interest in landscape that predominates. At the time of his birth, in 1775, there were two distinct traditions of landscape painting; the classical, or ideal, which originated in Italy with its ever-present evidence and atmosphere of the great historical past, and the naturalistic tradition, of which the Netherlandish artists were the leading exponents. On the Continent both these traditions reached their greatest heights in the seventeenth century, and made little progress in the eighteenth, but in Britain, which boasted few of its own painters in the seventeenth century, the eighteenth saw the influence of these traditions in the development of a native school of landscape painting, with Richard Wilson as the leading exponent of the classical tradition and Thomas Gainsborough of the naturalistic.

Wilson died in 1782 and Gainsborough in 1788, and thus when Turner became a student it was largely in the fields of topographical draughtsmanship and water-colour painting that the landscape school was being kept alive, by artists such as J. R. Cozens, Paul Sandby, Michelangelo Rooker, Joseph Farington and Edward Dayes. The sum of Turner's genius and achievement was that he succeeded in bringing together these traditions, and extracted from them all that he needed to create an entirely new style of landscape painting based on a deep understanding of light and form. Turner's highly individual atmospheric and romantic landscape painting developed gradually but consistently, and was in many ways far ahead of its time. Together with Constable's contemporary and equally important evolution of the naturalistic tradition, it became a significant force in European art of the nineteenth century. In Constable and Turner England has two of the greatest landscape painters of all time, and through them she has played a vital part in the history of nineteenth century art, particularly in the growth of Impressionism.

JOSEPH MALLORD WILLIAM TURNER was born on St George's Day, the 23rd of April 1775, the first child of William Turner, a barber of Maiden Lane in London, where he spent his early years. As the Redgrave brothers have written: 'His birthplace, and the scenes among which Turner passed his childhood, may be thought not to be best fitted to form a landscape painter, or to fill his youthful mind with images of beauty.' Yet Turner's artistic inclinations were soon in evidence, and he spent much of his time drawing. His earliest recorded drawing is dated 1787, and is a copy of the topographical engraving after a drawing by Michelangelo Rooker published as the head-piece of the *Oxford Almanack* for 1780. Of about the same date are two drawings copied from aquatints by the Reverend William Gilpin, a leading exponent of the picturesque, whose *Tours* were then much in vogue. Another early drawing is copied from an aquatint by Paul Sandby, while the earliest surviving sketches from nature were drawn in and around Oxford in 1789, at the end of which year Turner commenced his studies at the Royal Academy Schools. It seems likely that at

about the same time he was also taking lessons with one of the leading architectural draughtsmen of the day, Thomas Malton, whose influence is much in evidence in the first work that the young artist exhibited at the Royal Academy, in 1790. Thus by the time he was fifteen Turner had already shown himself to be fully aware of most of the leading elements in the artistic world of his day, and in the next ten years he was to prove his masterly assimilation of all these influences.

Turner now developed rapidly as a topographical water-colour artist of great ability. In 1791 he travelled to Bristol, where he was fascinated by the wild scenery of the Avon Gorge. This was the first of numerous journeys to all parts of Britain, on which Turner sketched profusely, with the growing demand for his topographical drawings and prints in mind. But at this stage his work was very much in line with that of his contemporary artists pursuing a similar career, most notable among whom was Thomas Girtin, his senior by only two months. Turner and Girtin, who worked together for the amiable Dr Monro when he employed them to make copies of drawings by J. R. Cozens and others, were close friends, and it will always remain one of the unanswerable questions in the history of English art, whether Girtin, had he not died as early as 1802, would have become as great an artist as

1. *Christ Church from the Meadows*. About 1798. Water-colours; 12⅜ × 17⅝ ins. Ashmolean Museum.

Turner did. That Turner was the more ambitious of the two is definite, for, with his election to the Royal Academy in mind, he began to paint in oils (an essential qualification), and the first of his works in that medium was exhibited in 1796. Entitled *Fishermen at Sea*, this painting is early evidence of Turner's predilection for subjects connected with the sea, which provided him with the best scope for his inspired rendering of atmosphere and light. But Turner did not neglect his water-colours, and it was these, rather than his oils, that gained the admiration of the critics at the Academy exhibitions of 1797 and the following two years. He now had more commissions for drawings than he could cope with, among them one for the *Oxford Almanack* from the Delegates of the Clarendon Press. The earliest of these ten *Almanack* drawings, *Christ Church from the Meadows*, which most probably dates from 1798, is reproduced here (plate 1). With its harmonious colours and its skilful draughtsmanship and composition, in which the sky and the water play such an important part, it is an excellent example of Turner's achievement at this time, and shows him to have been an outstanding figure among the water-colour artists of the closing years of the eighteenth century.

In the late autumn of 1799 Turner achieved his ambition, and was elected an Associate of the Royal Academy. Earlier that year he had been among the many visitors to William Beckford's London house, to see the two famous Altieri Claudes, which had just come to England. Now in the collection of Lord Fairhaven, these were among the first of the many masterpieces by Claude Lorrain that were to enter English collections at this period, and it is certain that Turner was strongly influenced by these examples of the great French landscape painter's art. A well-known illustration of this influence is a painting which he showed at the Royal Academy in 1803, *Macon: the Feast of the Opening of the Vintage*, which is now in the Sheffield City Art Gallery. One of the leading patrons and collectors of the day, Sir George Beaumont, said of this work that it was 'borrowed from Claude but the colouring forgotten'. Today it gives a very dark impression, but the bold freedom of the painting of the middle distance and the distance remains remarkable, while it also displays Turner's complete mastery of landscape composition in the grand classical manner. His adaptation of Richard Wilson's style in this tradition is seen in the *Aeneas with the Sibyl: Lake Avernus*, at the Tate Gallery, which dates from about 1800. There are also canvases which show the influence of Nicolas Poussin and Salvator Rosa, but of Rubens's landscapes, which were to have such a powerful effect on Constable, Turner did not approve. Indeed in one of his lectures some years later he said of him,

2. *Calais Pier: an English Packet arriving*. Exhibited 1803. Oil on canvas; $67\frac{3}{4} \times 94\frac{1}{2}$ ins. Tate Gallery.

that he 'threw around his tints like a bunch of flowers . . . obtaining everything by primitive colour, form and execution'.

All these artists were richly represented in English collections at this time, as were the Dutch painters whom Turner copied in his early years. The calm and glowing landscapes of Cuyp and the atmospheric seascapes of the Van de Veldes were clearly among his favourites. The influence of such marine paintings is seen in *Calais Pier: an English Packet arriving* (plate 2), which was also shown at the R.A. in 1803, when it was received with considerable adverse criticism. Here Turner already displays his skilful painting of the sea, and his ability to create a balanced composition by means of a subtle light effect. Raging sea and stormy sky are linked by the play of light on the boats and the figures. The idea for this painting came to Turner when he crossed the Channel for the first time, in very boisterous weather, in July 1802.

In addition to the influence of these great seventeenth century landscape and marine painters, another powerful force was affecting Turner. This was the assimilation of the English landscape around him during his travels throughout the British Isles. As yet it was largely in the medium of water-colours that he recorded what he had seen, but there are also several early oil paintings of scenes in England.

One such is the *View on Clapham Common* of about 1802 (plate 3), which combines a somewhat classical approach with accurate observation of the spot shown. This small canvas gives a foretaste of the series which Turner executed in about 1807 of 'pure' landscapes painted on the spot at various points on the river Thames between Walton and Windsor, and on the river Wey. *Eton, from the River* (plate 4) and *House beside River, with Trees and Sheep* (plate 5) both belong to this series, which forms part of the Turner Bequest at the Tate Gallery. Turner was anticipating Constable by some ten years in really grasping the character and beauty of the English landscape, seen at its most tranquil and satisfying in the valley of the Thames. These freely painted sketches have nothing forced or unnatural. The light effects usually rely on contrasts, and in nearly every painting the water is a vital element of the composition. Turner was breaking new ground in these paintings, for he allowed his vision of nature to dominate and control his work, though he never forgot the rules of composition which he had learnt from his close study of the old masters.

By 1810 Turner's position as the leading landscape painter of his day, both in oils and in water-colours, was fully established. In 1802 he had been elected a Royal Academician. That year the Peace of Amiens enabled him to make his first journey

3. *View on Clapham Common*. About 1802. Oil on canvas; 12 × 17 ins. Tate Gallery.

4. *Eton, from the River*. About 1807. Oil on thin veneer; 14 × 26 ins. Tate Gallery.

abroad, and he spent some five months in France and Switzerland. The two chief results of this journey, which were reflected in his Academy exhibits of the following year, were a lasting love for Alpine scenery, and a still closer appreciation of the works of his greatest predecessors through his prolonged visits to the Louvre.

In 1804 Turner opened his own gallery, in Queen Anne Street, off Harley Street, which was described in Farington's Diary as being '70 feet long and 20 wide'. Turner showed a group of paintings and water-colours, perhaps including the *Macon*, and this was to be the first of a considerable number of annual exhibitions in this gallery, which was rebuilt between 1819 and 1822. The premises at Queen Anne Street were retained by Turner until his death, and in his later years many of his finest works packed the gallery, which was suffering increasingly from neglect and damp. At the time of his funeral it was described by Richard Redgrave as 'dingy and dirty in the extreme . . . the pictures themselves . . . were dropping from their canvases'. Nevertheless Turner proved his unique position among English artists by retaining his own gallery in London for nearly half a century.

While only relatively few people could see Turner's paintings and drawings in his own gallery, at the Royal Academy or in other exhibitions, a far larger public was growing familiar with the artist through his engraved work, and in 1806 Turner was persuaded to undertake a project which was further to enhance his reputation. Inspired by Claude's *Liber Veritatis*, which had been most successfully engraved by Earlom some thirty years earlier, Turner began work on his own *Liber Studiorum*, the first part of which was issued in 1807, while further parts appeared at intervals until 1816. In the ninety-nine mezzotint plates of this series Turner again showed his remarkable versatility in adapting the most popular styles of his day, and the compositions range from country scenes in the manner of George Morland to landscapes in the grandest Claudian tradition. In 1794 the first two engravings after Turner's drawings had been published in *The Copper-Plate Magazine*, and by the time of his death he had produced some eight hundred engravings in various techniques. Most of these were illustrations for topographical works, such as *Picturesque Views in England and Wales* and the famous *Rivers of France*, while others were for the Annuals so popular at this time, or for special editions of the writings of men such as Walter Scott and Samuel Rogers. That the engravings of his drawings and paintings did much to enhance Turner's reputation is borne out by the comments of Dr Waagen, the German museum director whose records of English collections and

5. *House beside River, with Trees and Sheep*. About 1807. Oil on canvas; 38 × 45 ins. Tate Gallery.

art are an invaluable source of information. Writing of the Academy exhibition during his first visit to England in 1835, he tells us that he made a point 'of looking for the landscapes of the favourite painter, Turner, who is known throughout Europe by his numerous, often very clever, compositions for annuals and other books, where they appear in beautiful steel engravings'.

Another important event in Turner's life also took place in 1807, for in December of that year he was elected Professor of Perspective at the Royal Academy, an office which he retained until 1838. In fact he did not deliver his first lecture until over three years after his election, and he was never a very inspiring nor regular lecturer. However, despite his shortcomings the Academy felt reluctant to relieve Turner of the post because of their regard for him as an artist. Though the many enigmas of Turner's character still await clarification in a convincing biography, it is clear that throughout his life he retained the respect and admiration of most of his fellow-artists, and was rightly held by these to be the greatest among them. He cannot have been an easy colleague, but from the host of contradictory anecdotes of which he is the central figure he emerges as a kindly, sincere and thoughtful one, and he always retained an influential position. It is unfortunate that Turner's first biographer, Walter Thornbury, whose book appeared ten years after the artist's death, should have concentrated so much on the seamy and grasping side of his character. It is even more to be regretted that a really balanced survey is still lacking, for though A. J. Finberg's admirable *Life*, of which a second edition was published in 1961, provides a reliable account of the facts, it does not give its reader a living picture of Turner, either as a man or as an artist. The latter shortcoming can be made good by looking at Turner's paintings and drawings, but the former remains a very real obstacle in coming to a proper understanding of England's greatest painter.

AS WE HAVE seen, by 1810 Turner had already more than proved himself as a master in all spheres of landscape painting. In the next decade he was to adapt and develop his own style, and to look back somewhat less to the traditions and mannerisms of earlier artists. The very beautiful *Somer Hill*, shown at the R.A. in 1811 and now to be seen in the National Gallery of Scotland, is a well-preserved example of Turner's adaptation of the traditional 'country house portrait' into an effective landscape painting, imbued with subtle light and atmosphere. Of seven new landscape paintings shown in his own gallery in 1812, the critic of the *Sun* wrote: 'All these

17

6. *Snowstorm: Hannibal and his Army crossing the Alps.* Exhibited 1812. Oil on canvas; 57 × 93 ins. Tate Gallery.

pictures are painted with a boldness, vigour and truth which entitle the artist to a very high station among the landscape painters of any period.' These seven were again pure landscape paintings, while of the three canvases shown at the Royal Academy in the same year, one – the *View of High Street, Oxford*, now in the Loyd Collection at Lockinge – is straightforward topography, while another – *Snowstorm: Hannibal and his Army crossing the Alps* (plate 6) – is an outstanding example of his successful merging of landscape and historical painting. It seems that Turner thought of this subject during a storm which he experienced in Yorkshire. The figures play a minor part, though they help to emphasize the tremendous force of the storm's onslaught on the massive rocks of the Alpine pass.

Of an entirely different character is *Dido building Carthage, or the Rise of the Carthaginian Empire* (plate 7), which was one of two extremely Claudian compositions shown at the Royal Academy in 1815, the other being *Crossing the Brook*. These two were received with tremendous enthusiasm by artists, press and public, and in this year Turner was hailed as 'the greatest of all living geniuses' by a fellow-artist, Thomas Uwins. However, Sir George Beaumont, who had already shown himself a severe critic of Turner's work, thought both pictures poor, and at this time established his position as the chief opponent of Turner's developments of landscape painting, which, quite rightly, he considered to be endangering the classical tradition of which he was an avowed supporter. *Dido building Carthage* is, in fact, closely linked with Claude's *Seaport: Embarkation of the Queen of Sheba*, then in the Angerstein Collection. Even after the recent cleaning of the Turner it is difficult, however, to agree today with the critic of the *St James's Chronicle*, that 'this is a fine work which, in grandeur and ideal beauty, Claude never equalled', though in many details, especially in the foreground, it is most impressive. (The reproduction here has unfortunately had to be made from a photograph taken before the restoration.) In 1824 the Angerstein Collection was purchased for the nation as the foundation of the National Gallery, and Turner bequeathed *Dido building Carthage* and the *Sun rising through Vapour* of 1807 to the nation, on condition that they were hung 'in perpetuity' between two of the Angerstein Claudes, the *Seaport* and the *Landscape: Marriage of Isaac and Rebecca*. When the time came the pictures were accepted on this condition, and were hung beside the Claudes for a good many years, but today this is no longer the case.

A painting that happily remains in excellent condition is *Dort or Dordrecht: the Dort Packet-Boat from Rotterdam becalmed* (plate 8), which was one of three

7. *Dido building Carthage, or the Rise of the Carthaginian Empire*. Exhibited 1815.
Oil on canvas; $61\frac{1}{4} \times 91\frac{1}{4}$ ins. National Gallery.

8. *Dort or Dordrecht: The Dort Packet-Boat from Rotterdam becalmed.* Exhibited 1818.
Oil on canvas; 62 × 92 ins. Major le G. G. W. Horton-Fawkes, Farnley Hall.

shown at the Academy in 1818. It was purchased at the exhibition for 500 guineas by Walter Fawkes, of Farnley Hall in Yorkshire, and today it is still in the possession of the Fawkes family at Farnley. Walter Fawkes had been buying Turner's paintings and water-colours since the early years of the century, and in 1810 the artist paid his first visit to Farnley Hall, a beautiful house splendidly situated overlooking the valley of the Wharfe. Here Turner was to spend some of his happiest days, and though much of Walter Fawkes's collection has been dispersed there are still many mementoes of Turner at Farnley. Among these is a series of twenty-nine drawings in water-colour and body-colour of scenes inside and outside the house, and of views in the surrounding country. There is also an album of scintillating small water-colours of birds, including a delightful robin, a glittering kingfisher and the noble head of a peacock. At Farnley today one can still sense the presence of Turner, and knowing how welcome and loved he was in these beautiful surroundings it is all the more difficult to credit the disreputable picture of his character which Thornbury and his followers have spread. Thus it is fitting that Turner's major work still at Farnley, the *Dort*, should be one of the artist's most serene sea paintings, in which there is not the slightest element of tension or storm, for it is imbued with an atmos-

phere of supreme beauty and complete calm.

In 1819 Turner's reputation was still further advanced by the public exhibitions of two private collections. In March Sir John Leicester, another of the principal collectors and patrons of the time, opened his gallery in Hill Street, where eight of Turner's oil paintings were to be seen. In April, Mr Fawkes, encouraged by the success of Sir John's exhibition, showed his large collection of English water-colours at his town house in Grosvenor Place. This included over eighty drawings by Turner, most of which had not been exhibited before. Both exhibitions were extremely well received, and the press again commented most favourably on Turner's achievements. But this year saw an even more significant event in the artist's career, for at the beginning of August he set out for his first visit to Italy.

Until the restrictions on travel in the period following the French Revolution it had been customary for most British artists to visit Italy as an essential part of their training, but so far Turner had only been to France, Switzerland and Germany. Now he was to spend some five months in Italy, visiting Turin, Venice, Bologna, Rome, Naples, Salerno and Florence. During his travels he made many hundreds of pencil sketches which provided him with an ample storehouse of topographical

9. *Chichester Channel.* 1829. Oil on canvas; 25 × 53½ ins. Tate Gallery.

information, and in future years scenes in Italy, and especially in Venice, were to be among his favourite subjects. Now at last he was able to familiarize himself with the landscape which had inspired Claude, Poussin, Salvator Rosa, Wilson and the other painters in the classical tradition. He also saw the masterpieces of earlier Italian painting, and absorbed the artistic and historic atmosphere of Italy's greatest cities. Turner tried to express all these experiences in the vast canvas which he showed at the R.A. in 1820, *Rome from the Vatican: Raffaelle, accompanied by La Fornarina, preparing his Pictures for the Decoration of the Loggia*, but this over-crowded composition was a failure, and a happier product of the journey was the series of water-colours, most of which were acquired by Mr Fawkes.

In these water-colours Turner displayed a heightened sense of colour, and this is also evident in the luminous *Bay of Baiae, with Apollo and the Sibyl* (plate 10), which was exhibited in 1823. Here, as in many of his later oil paintings, Turner's great skill and experience as a water-colour artist has clearly affected his technique in oils, which now becomes increasingly fluid and often almost translucent, though the beautiful foreground details still retain a very firm character. Another example of this development in his painting in the 1820's is the mellow *Chichester Channel* of 1829 (plate 9), which reminds one of the series of river landscapes painted on the spot in about 1807, and which like most of these is unfinished, being a study for a picture of the same size at Petworth. From these examples it will be seen that it was the clear light and vivid colours of Italy, rather than the classical traditions of that country, which had a strong influence on Turner. Indeed his visit may be said to have provided the impetus he needed to achieve his ultimate emancipation from the various traditions which had so far provided the basis of his work. Now, with all his studies and experience behind him, he was able to give rein to his own individual style – to capture the superb effects of light and form – to create the magnificent canvases and water-colours by which he earned his place as one of the greatest artists of all time.

THIS PROCESS OF emancipation can be traced throughout the 1820's, though it is not often evident in the exhibited paintings, which still show the old influences, and occasionally also new ones. In *Boccaccio relating the Tale of the Birdcage*, which was shown at the Royal Academy in 1828, the figures are very similar to those in the works of Thomas Stothard, a fellow-academician who was twenty years older than Turner, and who had himself been strongly influenced by the figure paintings of Antoine Watteau. Indeed Turner was also directly influenced by Watteau, as is borne out by the fact that in about 1831 he painted *Watteau Painting*, while he is said to have made a copy of Watteau's famous *Les Plaisirs du Bal* at the Dulwich Gallery in 1832. One of the large subject paintings of the late 1830's, *Phryne going to the Public Baths as Venus· Demosthenes taunted by Aeschines*, which was exhibited in 1838, is an example of the continued use of such Watteau-like figures, but in this somewhat theatrical composition Turner has incorporated a beautiful and freely painted landscape in the middle distance.

10. *The Bay of Baiae, with Apollo and the Sibyl*. Exhibited 1823. Oil on canvas; $57\frac{1}{2} \times 93\frac{1}{2}$ ins. Tate Gallery.

11. *Rocky Bay with Figures*. About 1830. Oil on canvas; 35½ × 48½ ins. Tate Gallery.

Rocky Bay with Figures (plate 11), which was painted in about 1830, is an outstanding example of the great advances made in his landscape painting during these years, and it should be remembered that he was already in his fifties at this time. With a relatively limited range of colours this canvas achieves a wonderful feeling of realistic atmosphere. Combining passages of exceptionally thick paint with others which are almost translucent, Turner has built up a composition of light and mass which provides a very complete picture of this particular spot, probably on the Mediterranean coast, though perhaps purely imaginary. Such a work is the fruit of years of the closest observation of nature and of patient study of the canvases of earlier artists, for even in this essentially individual Turner there is still an echo of Claude.

Mr Walter Fawkes had died in 1825, but his special place among Turner's patrons was now filled by the growing friendship of George Wyndham, third Earl of Egremont. The Earl, who was born in 1751, had bought his first painting by Turner, *The Egremont Seapiece*, as early as 1802, and in 1809 he had commissioned views of Petworth, his beautiful house in Sussex. But it was not until after the death of his father in 1829 that Turner became a regular and frequent visitor to Petworth, where he was given his own painting room. Lord Egremont was a judicious collector and a sympathetic patron, and in his house Turner was able to be entirely at his ease and to paint to his heart's content. A group of remarkably free 'impressionistic' interiors at Petworth, in water-colour and body-colour on blue paper, provide a further insight into Turner's concern with problems of light, as do the one or two oil paintings of similar interiors, among them the *Music Party, Petworth* (plate 12), which, like all these works, was executed some time between 1830 and 1837, the year of the Earl's death. In these interiors Turner gives the barest indications of the forms and figures, but relies on the combination of colour and mass to achieve the impression which he is trying to record. He was also inspired by the beauty of the park and the country surrounding the house, and some of the paintings of this scenery are among the most poetic of his realistic landscapes. Today twenty of Turner's paintings collected by the third Earl of Egremont are still at Petworth, now the property of the National Trust, and they provide a fascinating survey of the painter's development up to the middle 1830's.

Though Turner's exhibited paintings were not then receiving the general acclaim which had been usual in the first twenty-five years of the century, his reputation was more than kept alive by his engraved work. In 1826 Turner had begun the *Picturesque*

27

12. *Music Party, Petworth*. About 1830–37. Oil on canvas; 48 × 35½ ins. Tate Gallery.

Views in England and Wales, for which he was to complete over ninety illustrations, published between 1827 and 1838. This series, however, was a financial failure – three publishers in turn failed to make a success of it – and there were few subscribers or purchasers. In complete contrast was the tremendous acclaim with which the *de luxe* editions of Samuel Rogers's *Italy* and *Poems* were received in 1830 and 1834 respectively. Among the illustrations in the former were twenty-five vignettes after drawings by Turner, and in the latter there were thirty-three such engravings. In the 1830's Turner also carried out commissions for illustrations to the works of Scott, Byron, Milton and others. Outstanding among these series of small illustrations are those for *The Rivers of France*, the first part of which, with twenty-five engravings devoted to the Loire, was published in 1833, while the two parts dealing with the river Seine appeared in 1834 and 1835. Nearly all these hundreds of engravings were executed from highly finished water-colour drawings, and Turner was always careful to exercise close supervision over the engravers working on them. Considering the great volume of work these undertakings must have involved for the painter, it is hardly surprising that to a certain extent the progress of his art in the 1830's was disappointing. But as the drawing of *Blois* (plate 13) shows, Turner was

13. *Blois*. 1832. Water-colours and body-colours on blue-grey paper; $5\frac{3}{8} \times 7\frac{1}{4}$ ins. Ashmolean Museum.

14. *Bridge of Sighs, Ducal Palace and Custom-house, Venice; Canaletti painting.* Exhibited 1833.
Oil on wood; 20 × 32 ins. Tate Gallery.

15. *Venice, the Grand Canal*. About 1840. Water-colours; $8\frac{1}{2} \times 12\frac{3}{8}$ ins. Ashmolean Museum.

at the height of his powers in water-colours. Combining vivid colours with delicate outlines, such drawings revolutionized the developments in this medium. The *Blois*, which dates from 1832, is one of a group of twenty-four drawings for *The Rivers of France* which belonged to John Ruskin and which he presented to the Ashmolean Museum, Oxford, while over two hundred more are in the British Museum.

It has been said that Turner was first and foremost a water-colourist, and that his most successful oil paintings are those in which he adapted the freedom and fluidity of colour and line which his experience in water-colours had taught him. A painting which illustrates this theory to some extent is *Bridge of Sighs, Ducal Palace and Custom-house, Venice: Canaletti painting* (plate 14). Shown at the Royal Academy in 1833 this was one of the first two oil paintings of Venice exhibited by Turner. In the following years, until 1846, this inspiring city featured frequently and regularly in his exhibited works. 'Canaletti Painting' – the somewhat ludicrous and theatrical figure seen in the left foreground – plays no essential role in this composition, though his inclusion is a sign of Turner's respect for one of the greatest of his predecessors among the painters of the Venetian scene. But there is a world of difference between Canaletto's detailed architectural compositions and Turner's vivid rendering of the city's wonderful wealth of colour and light. In Venice, with its unique combination of buildings and water, Turner felt liberated, and though he visited the city only three times – in 1819, 1835 and 1840 – it clearly meant a great deal to him. From the numerous rapid pencil sketches made during his first visit, to such brilliant water-colours as *The Grand Canal* (plate 15), which captures the essence of the place with breathtaking delicacy and economy, Turner is at his best when depicting Venice, and it must rank with Farnley and Petworth as one of the places where he was freely able to develop the calmer and more placid elements of his art.

During the same years he was also continuing his development as the painter of scenes of tension and drama, such as the *Calais Pier* (plate 2) and the *Snowstorm* (plate 6) had shown him to be from the beginning. *A Fire at Sea* (plate 16), which is an unfinished work of about 1834, is one of the greatest of his later paintings in this vein. Sea, sky and figures are here combined to make a composition full of power and movement, in which colour plays a very minor part. On 16th October 1834, the Houses of Parliament were burnt down. This event provided a perfect subject for Turner, and in the following year he exhibited *The Burning of the House of Lords and Commons*, which is now in the Cleveland Museum. This painting, with its brilliant colours

16. *A Fire at Sea*. About 1834. Oil on canvas; $67\frac{1}{2} \times 86\frac{1}{2}$ ins. National Gallery.

17. *Sunrise: A Castle on a Bay*. About 1840. Oil on canvas; $35\frac{1}{2} \times 47\frac{1}{2}$ ins. Tate Gallery.

and magnificent rendering of water, sky and flames, was exceptionally well received by the critics that year. As has been vividly recorded by the painter, E. V. Rippingille, it was one of the canvases which Turner repainted almost entirely at the Royal Academy on varnishing day. When sent in to the exhibition it was 'a mere daub of several colours . . . like chaos before the creation . . . Turner, for the three hours I was there,' wrote Rippingille, 'and I understood it had been the same since he began in the morning – never ceased to work, or even once looked or turned from the wall on which his picture hung. . . . A small box of colours, a few very small brushes, and a vial or two, were at his feet. . . . In one part of the mysterious proceedings Turner, who worked almost entirely with his palette knife, was observed to be rolling and spreading a lump of half-transparent stuff over his picture, the size of a finger in length and thickness. . . . Presently the work was finished: Turner gathered his tools together . . . and then, with his face still turned to the wall, and at the same distance from it, went sideling off, without speaking a word to anybody. . . . All looked with a half-wondering smile, and Maclise, who stood near, remarked, "There, that's masterly, he does not stop to look at his work; he *knows* it is done, and he is off".' Such unorthodox methods did nothing to enhance Turner's reputation with the public, and the poor condition of many of his canvases today reflects the reckless way in which he often worked.

Also in America, at the Museum of Fine Arts in Boston, is the famous *Slave Ship*, exhibited in 1840. This is one of Turner's most forceful romantic canvases, instinct with drama and depth of feeling. It was given by his father to John Ruskin, who wrote of it, 'I believe, if I were reduced to rest Turner's immortality upon any single work, I would choose this'. But in 1869 he sold it, the subject having 'become too painful to live with'.

In many of his storm scenes Turner achieves a concentric composition by introducing a kind of whirlwind. We see this in the *Snowstorm* of 1812 (plate 6), and again in a painting exhibited in 1842 with the lengthy title, *Snow Storm – steam-boat off a harbour's mouth making signals in shallow water, and going by the lead. The author was in this storm on the night the Ariel left Harwich*. This is a swirling symphony of greys and whites, with touches of yellow, which one critic at the time of its exhibition declared to be merely a 'mass of soapsuds and whitewash'. Turner himself had said of the painting and the experience which inspired it, 'I did not expect to escape, but I felt bound to record it if I did. But no one had any business to like it'. The whirlwind theme is found again in *Light and Colour (Goethe's*

Theory), one of a pair of octagonal canvases shown at the Royal Academy in 1843, and it seems that these whirlwinds must have had some special meaning for Turner.

1843 was the year of the anonymous publication of the first volume of John Ruskin's *Modern Painters*. The second volume appeared in 1846, the third and fourth in 1856 and the fifth in 1860. While an undergraduate at Oxford Ruskin had been much affected by the constant adverse criticism which Turner's works attracted at this time. Dedicated to the 'Landscape Artists of England', *Modern Painters* is in fact a monumental defence of Turner, of whose work Ruskin was already a great admirer, when he met the artist for the first time in 1840, recording in his diary: 'Introduced today to the man who beyond all doubt is the greatest of the age; greatest in every faculty of the imagination, in every branch of scenic knowledge; at once *the* painter and poet of the day, J. M. W. Turner. Everybody had described him to me as coarse, boorish, unintellectual, vulgar. This I knew to be impossible. I found in him a somewhat eccentric, keen-mannered, matter-of-fact, English-minded-gentleman: good-natured evidently, bad-tempered evidently, hating humbug of all sorts, shrewd, perhaps a little selfish, highly intellectual, the powers of his mind not brought out with any delight in their manifestation, or intention of dis-

play, but flashing out occasionally in a word or a look.' Despite frequent exaggeration and the use of debatable generalizations, *Modern Painters* is one of the most penetrating works ever written in defence of an artist, and the first volume was quickly influential in restoring to Turner some of the respect and admiration which had earlier been his. It laid the foundations for the understanding of Turner's later work, which is today considered as the greatest flowering of his genius, but which at the time of its execution was, quite understandably as it was so much ahead of its time, more often derided than appreciated.

In his water-colour portrait (plate 20) J. T. Smith, who was Keeper of Prints and Drawings at the British Museum, shows Turner as a somewhat ordinary and far from handsome man, and this portrayal is borne out by the description of him in Samuel and Richard Redgrave's *A Century of British Painters*, first published in 1866: 'In person Turner had little of the outward appearance that we love to attribute to the possessors of genius. In the last twenty years of his life, during which we knew him well, his short figure had become corpulent – his face, perhaps from continual exposure to the air, was unusually red, and a little inclined to blotches. His dark eye was bright and restless – his nose, aquiline. He generally wore what is called a black dress-coat,

18. *Rain, Steam and Speed – The Great Western Railway*. Exhibited 1844. Oil on canvas; 35¾ × 48 ins. National Gallery.

which would have been the better for brushing – the sleeves were mostly too long, coming down over his fat and not over-clean hands. He wore his hat while painting on the varnishing days – or otherwise a large wrapper over his head.'

RUSKIN CONTINUALLY EMPHASIZES Turner's qualities as a truthful painter of nature. This judgment is well borne out by many of the numerous paintings which Turner never exhibited, and which make no attempt to depict a specific subject. One such, dating from about 1840, is *Waves breaking against the Wind* (plate 19), which is the fruit of his close observation and love of the sea. It is not impossible that this wonderful study of waves was painted on the spot, and it is certain that in such entirely unfettered paintings Turner was most truly himself. *Sunrise: A Castle on a Bay* (plate 17) comes in the same category and probably dates from about the same time. In contrast to the force and movement of the sea painting, this shows Turner in the calmest of moods, his eye thrilled by the beauty of the sunrise, and his brush evoking it with a wonderful combination of colour and form, and with a perfect understanding of the problems of light involved. Studies such as this often served him as the basis of his more complex exhibited paintings. The most famous of

these fluid landscape impressions is the *Norham Castle, Sunrise*, which, with its delicate touches of pink, blue and yellow, ranks as one of the very greatest of Turner's paintings.

It was canvases such as these that crowded Turner's gallery in Queen Anne Street during the last years of his life. They were personal records which the artist had no desire to sell. On the other hand, *Rain, Steam and Speed – the Great Western Railway* (plate 18), which was shown at the Academy in 1844, also never found a buyer. This was one of the outstanding examples of Turner's mastery of the problems of light, colour and form, and over thirty years elapsed before any other artist was able to come anywhere near his solution of these all-important problems.

J. M. W. Turner died on 19th December 1851, in his seventy-seventh year. His funeral was a most dismal affair, and his fellow-artists were appalled at the terrible state of the numerous paintings and drawings crammed into the dilapidated gallery in Queen Anne Street. Turner left an elaborate will, by which the very considerable fortune that his work had brought him was to be largely devoted to the relief of aged and distressed artists. However, the will was successfully disputed by relatives, and as a result Turner's scheme for a special gallery to house his remaining works was also thwarted.

19. *Waves breaking against the Wind*. About 1840. Oil on canvas; 23 × 35 ins. Tate Gallery.

20. *J. M. W. Turner in the Print Room of the British Museum*, by J. T. Smith (1766–1833). Water-colours over pencil; 8¾ × 7¼ ins. British Museum.

Instead these became the property of the nation, and, in addition to the two paintings specifically bequeathed to the National Gallery, the national collections were enriched by some three hundred paintings and over nineteen thousand drawings. Since 1856, when these were handed over to the authorities of the National Gallery, the adequate housing of this unique collection has caused great problems. Today, thanks to the munificence of Lord Duveen, there are several galleries at the Tate Gallery devoted entirely to Turner's paintings, and a small selection of the Turner Bequest is usually on view at the National Gallery. The drawings are now deposited in the Print Room of the British Museum, where students and others can see them on request. In recent years good progress has been made in cleaning some of the paintings, and the Turner galleries at the Tate are now a splendid memorial to this great, but often misunderstood, artist. He himself would have been especially pleased to find his paintings exhibited so near the river Thames, which meant so much to him.

ARMSTRONG, SIR WALTER, *Turner*. T. Agnew and Sons, 1902.

BELL, C. F., *The Exhibited Works of J. M. W. Turner, R.A.* George Bell and Sons, 1901.

FINBERG, A. J., *Complete Inventory of the Drawings of the Turner Bequest, arranged chronologically*, 2 vols. H.M. Stationery Office, 1909.
Turner's Sketches and Drawings. Methuen and Co, 1910.
In Venice with Turner, The Cotswold Gallery, 1930.
The Life of J. M. W. Turner. Oxford, Clarendon Press, first edition, 1939, second edition, 1961.

RAWLINSON, W. G., *Turner's 'Liber Studiorum'*. Macmillan and Co, second edition, 1906.
The Engraved Work of J. M. W. Turner, 2 vols. Macmillan and Co, 1908 and 1913.

REDGRAVE, R. and S., *A Century of British Painters*, 2 vols. Smith, Elder and Co, 1866. Phaidon Press Edition, 1947.

RUSKIN, JOHN, *Works* (Library Edition) edited by Cook and Wedderburn, 39 vols. George Allen, 1903–12.

THORNBURY, WALTER, *Life of J. M. W. Turner*, 2 vols. Hurst and Blackett, 1862. Second edition, 1877.

ACKNOWLEDGMENTS

All the Colour Plates and Plates 2, 3, 4, 6, 9, 11, 12 and 14, are reproduced by courtesy of the Trustees of the Tate Gallery, London. Plates 7, 16 and 18 are reproduced by courtesy of the Trustees of the National Gallery, London. Plate 20 is reproduced by courtesy of the Trustees of the British Museum, London. Plates 1, 13 and 15 are reproduced by courtesy of the Visitors of the Ashmolean Museum, Oxford. Plate 8 is reproduced by kind permission of Major le G. G. W. Horton-Fawkes, of Farnley Hall.